One of India's most cherished renaissance figures, Rabindranath Tagore (1861-1941) put us on the literary map of the world when his *Gitanjali* was awarded the Nobel Prize for literature in 1913. A poet's poet, he is a maker of not only modern Indian literature but also the modern Indian mind. Myriad-minded, he was a poet, short story writer, novelist, dramatist, essayist, painter and composer of songs. Gandhi called him the 'Great Sentinel'. His world-wide acclaim as a social, political, religious and aesthetic thinker, innovator in education and a champion of the 'One World' idea makes him a living presence.

Fruit Gathering was first published in 1916. Among the eighty-six poems contained in this book more than fifty are of religious temper collected from *Gitimala*, *Gitali*, *Utsarga*, *Kheya*, *Naivedya* and *Gitanjali*. The rest of the poems are from *Katha* and *Balaka*. The former contains ballad-like verses celebrating the courage, sacrifice and dedication of men and women from Indian history. The latter is marked with an opulence of imagery, metrical innovations and breadth of vision. In *Fruit Gathering*, these three varying styles merge and one is presented with a mystic Tagore with only one voice.

RABINDRA RACHANAVALI

Fruit Gathering

Rabindranath Tagore

Rupa . Co

Published 2003 by
Rupa & Co
7/16, Ansari Road, Daryaganj
New Delhi 110 002

Sales Centres:
Allahabad Bangalore Chandigarh Chennai
Dehradun Hyderabad Jaipur Kathmandu
Kolkata Ludhiana Mumbai Pune

Design & Typeset by
Arrt Creations
45 Nehru Apts, Kalkaji
New Delhi 110 019

Printed in India by
Gopsons Papers Ltd
A-14 Sector 60, Noida 201 301

Page ii: Rabindranath Tagore in Santiniketan,1932
Page vi: Unsigned. No date. Ink and watercolour on paper.

Contents

1

Bid me and I shall gather my fruits to bring them in full baskets into your courtyard, though some are lost and some not ripe.

For the season grows heavy with its fullness, and there is a plaintive shepherd's pipe in the shade.

Bid me and I shall set sail on the river.

The March wind is fretful, fretting the languid waves into murmurs.

The garden has yielded its all, and in the weary hour of evening the call comes from your house on the shore in the sunset.

2

My life when young was like a flower—a flower that loosens a petal or two from her abundance and never feels the loss when the spring breeze comes to beg at her door.

Now at the end of youth my life is like a fruit, having nothing to spare, and waiting to offer herself completely with her full burden of sweetness.

3

Is summer's festival only for fresh blossoms and not also for withered leaves and faded flowers?

Is the song of the sea in tune only with the rising waves?

Does it not also sing with the waves that fall?

Jewels are woven into the carpet where stands my king, but there are patient clods waiting to be touched by his feet.

Few are the wise and the great who sit by my Master, but he has taken the foolish in his arms and made me his servant for ever.

4

I woke and found his letter with the morning.

I do not know what it says, for I cannot read.

I shall leave the wise man alone with his books, I shall not trouble him, for who knows if he can read what the letter says.

Let me hold it to my forehead and press it to my heart.

When the night grows still and stars come out one by one I will spread it on my lap and stay silent.

The rustling leaves will read it aloud to me, the rushing stream will chant it, and the seven wise stars will sing it to me from the sky.

I cannot find what I seek, I cannot understand what I would learn: but this unread letter has lightened my burdens and turned my thoughts into songs.

5

A handful of dust could hide your signal when I did not know its meaning.
Now that I am wiser I read it in all that hid it before.
It is painted in petals of flowers; waves flash it from their foam; hills hold it high on their summits.
I had my face turned from you, therefore I read the letters awry and knew not their meaning.

6

Where roads are made I lose my way.

In the wide water, in the blue sky there is no line of a track.

The pathway is hidden by the birds' wings, by the star-fires, by the flowers of the wayfaring seasons.

And I ask my heart if its blood carries the wisdom of the unseen way.

7

Alas, I cannot stay in the house, and home has become no home to me, for the eternal Stranger calls, he is going along the road.

The sound of his footfall knocks at my breast; it pains me!

The wind is up, the sea is moaning.

I leave all my cares and doubts to follow the homeless tide, for the Stranger calls me, he is going along the road.

8

Be ready to launch forth, my heart! and let those linger who must.

For your name has been called in the morning sky.

Wait for none!

The desire of the bud is for the night and dew, but the blown flower cries for the freedom of light.

Burst your sheath, my heart, and come forth!

9

When I lingered among my hoarded treasure I felt like a worm that feeds in the dark upon the fruit where it was born.

I leave this prison of decay.

I care not to haunt the mouldy stillness, for I go in search of everlasting youth; I throw away all that is not one with my life nor as light as my laughter.

I run through time and, O my heart, in your chariot dances the poet who sings while he wanders.

10

You took my hand and drew me to your side, made me sit on the high seat before all men, till I became timid, unable to stir and walk my own way; doubting and debating at every step lest I should tread upon any thorn of their disfavour.

I am freed at last!
The blow has come, the drum of insult sounded, my seat is laid low in the dust.
My paths are open before me.

My wings are full of the desire of the sky.
I go to join the shooting stars of midnight, to plunge into the profound shadow.

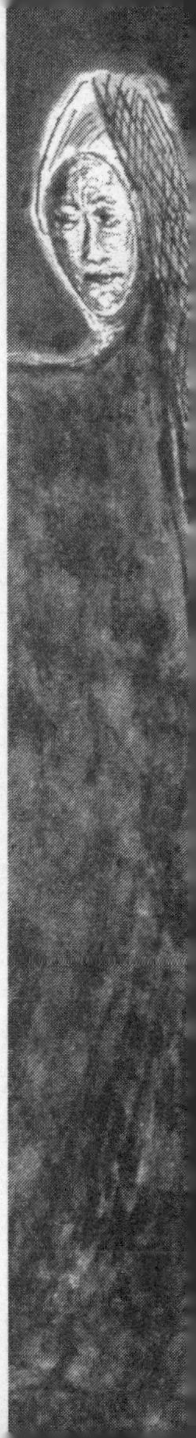

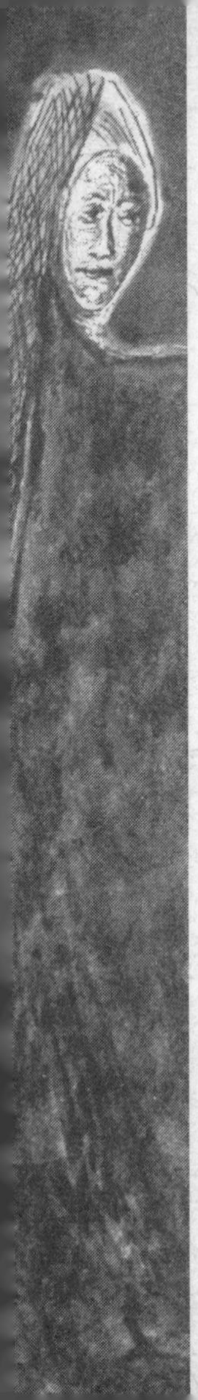

I am like the storm-driven cloud of summer that, having cast off its crown of gold, hangs as a sword the thunderbolt upon a chain of lightning.

In desperate joy I run upon the dusty path of the despised; I draw near to your final welcome.

The child finds its mother when it leaves her womb.

When I am parted from you, thrown out from your household, I am free to see your face.

11

It decks me only to mock me, this jewelled chain of mine.

It bruises me when on my neck, it strangles me when I struggle to tear it off.

It grips my throat, it chokes my singing.

Could I but offer it to your hand, my Lord, I would be saved.

Take it from me, and in exchange bind me to you with a garland, for I am ashamed to stand before you with this jewelled chain on my neck.

12

Far below flowed the Jumna, swift and clear, above frowned the jutting bank.

Hills dark with the woods and scarred with the torrents were gathered around.

Govinda, the great Sikh teacher, sat on the rock reading scriptures, when Raghunath, his disciple, proud of his wealth, came and bowed to him and said, 'I have brought my poor present unworthy of your acceptance.'

Thus saying he displayed before the teacher a pair of gold bangles wrought with costly stones.

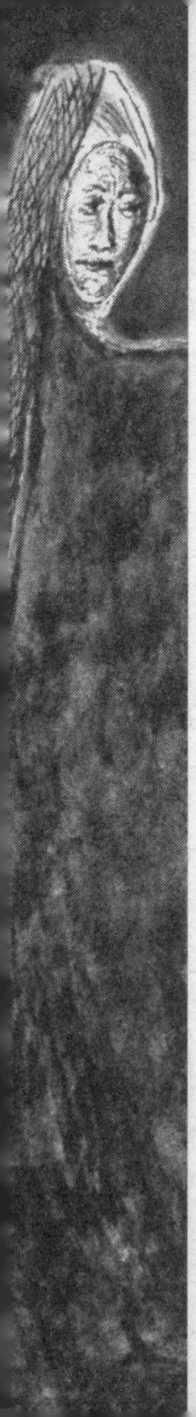

The master took up one of them, twirling it round his finger, and the diamonds darted shafts of light. Suddenly it slipped from his hand and rolled down the bank into the water.

'Alas,' screamed Raghunath and jumped into the stream.

The teacher set his eyes upon his book, and the water held and hid what it stole and went its way.

The daylight faded when Raghunath came back to the teacher tired and dripping.

He panted and said, 'I can still get it back if you show me where it fell.'

The teacher took up the remaining bangle and throwing it into the water said, 'It is there.'

13

To move is to meet you every moment, Fellow-traveller!

It is to sing to the falling of your feet.

He whom your breath touches does not glide by the shelter of the bank.

He spreads a reckless sail to the wind and rides the turbulent water.

He who throws his doors open and steps onward receives your greeting.

He does not stay to count his gain or to mourn his loss; his heart beats the drum for his march, for that is to march with you every step, Fellow-traveller!

14

My portion of the best in this world will come from your hands: such was your promise.

Therefore your light glistens in my tears.

I fear to be led by others lest I miss you waiting in some road corner to be my guide.

I walk my own wilful way till my very folly tempts you to my door.

For I have your promise that my portion of the best in this world will come from your hands.

15

Your speech is simple, my Master, but not theirs who talk of you.

I understand the voice of your stars and the silence of your trees. I know that my heart would open like a flower; that my life has filled itself at a hidden fountain.

Your songs, like birds from the lonely land of snow, are winging to build their nests in my heart against the warmth of its April, and I am content to wait for the merry season.

16

They knew the way and went to seek you along the narrow lane, but I wandered abroad into the night for I was ignorant.

I was not schooled enough to be afraid of you in the dark, therefore I came upon your doorstep unaware.

The wise rebuked me and bade me be gone, for I had not come by the lane.

I turned away in doubt, but you held me fast, and their scolding became louder every day.

17

I brought out my earthen lamp from my house and cried. 'Come, children, I will light your path!'

The night was still dark when I returned, leaving the road to its silence; crying, 'Light me, O Fire! for my earthen lamp lies broken in the dust!'

18

No: it is not yours to open buds into blossoms.

Shake the bud, strike it; it is beyond your power to make it blossom.

Your touch soils it, you tear its petals to pieces and strew them in the dust.

But no colours appear, and no perfume.

Ah! it is not for you to open the bud into a blossom.

He who can open the bud does it so simply.

He gives it a glance, and the life-sap stirs through its veins.

At his breath the flower spreads its wings and flutters in the wind.

Colours flush out like heart-longings, the perfume betrays a sweet secret.

He who can open the bud does it so simply.

19

Sudas, the gardener, plucked from his tank the last lotus left by the ravage of winter and went to sell it to the king at the palace gate.

There he met a traveller who said to him, 'Ask your price for the last lotus,–I shall offer it to Lord Buddha.'

Sudas said, 'If you pay one golden *masha* it will be yours.'

The traveller paid it.

At that moment the king came out and he wished to buy the flower, for he was on his way to see Lord Buddha, and he thought, 'It would be a fine thing to lay at his feet the lotus that bloomed in winter.'

When the gardener said he had been offered a golden *masha* the king offered him ten, but the traveller doubled the price.

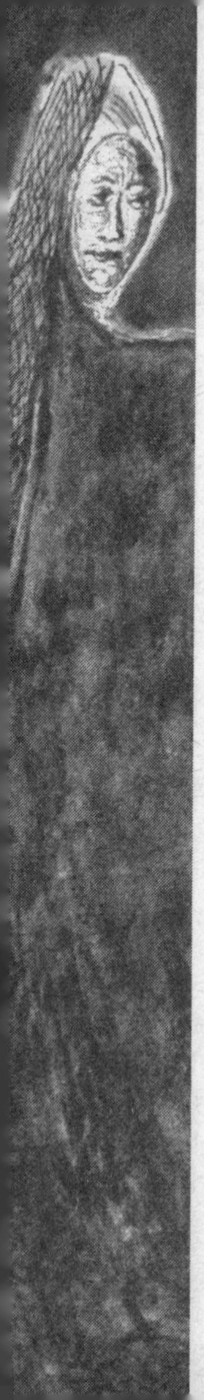

The gardener, being greedy, imagined a greater gain from him for whose sake they were bidding. He bowed and said, 'I cannot sell this lotus.'

In the hushed shade of the mango grove beyond the city wall Sudas stood before Lord Buddha, on whose lips sat the silence of love and whose eyes beamed peace like the morning star of the dew-washed autumn.

Sudas looked in his face and put the lotus at his feet and bowed his head to the dust.

Buddha smiled and asked, 'What is your wish, my son?'

Sudas cried, 'The least touch of your feet.'

20

Make me thy poet, O Night, veiled Night!

There are some who have sat speechless for ages in thy shadow; let me utter their songs.

Take me up on thy chariot without wheels, running noiselessly from world to world, thou queen in the palace of time, thou darkly beautiful!

Many a questioning mind has stealthily entered thy courtyard and roamed through thy lampless house seeking for answers.

From many a heart, pierced with the arrows of joy from the hands of the Unknown, have burst forth glad chants, shaking the darkness to its foundation.

Those wakeful souls gaze in the starlight in wonder at the treasure they have suddenly found.

Make me their poet, O Night, the poet of thy fathomless silence.

21

I will meet one day the Life within me, the joy that hides in my life, though the days perplex my path with their idle dust.

I have known it in glimpses, and its fitful breath has come upon me making my thoughts fragrant for a while.

I will meet one day the Joy without me that dwells behind the screen of light—and will stand in the overflowing solitude where all things are seen as by their creator.

22

This Autumn morning is tired with excess of light, and if your songs grow fitful and languid give me your flute awhile.

I shall but play with it as the whim takes me,—now take it on my lap, now touch it with my lips, now keep it by my side on the grass.

But in the solemn evening stillness I shall gather flowers, to deck it with wreaths, I shall fill it with fragrance; I shall worship it with the lighted lamp.

Then at night I shall come to you and give you back your flute.

You will play on it the music of midnight when the lonely crescent moon wanders among the stars.

23

The poet's mind floats and dances on the waves of life amidst the voices of wind and water.

Now when the sun has set and the darkened sky draws down upon the sea like drooping lashes upon a weary eye it is time to take away his pen, and let his thoughts sink into the bottom of the deep amid the eternal secret of that silence.

24

The night is dark and your slumber is deep in the hush of my being.

Wake, O Pain of Love, for I know not how to open the door, and I stand outside.

The hours wait, the stars watch, the wind is still, the silence is heavy in my heart.

Wake, Love, wake! Brim my empty cup, and with a breath of song ruffle the night.

25

The bird of the morning sings.

Whence has he word of the morning before the morning breaks, and when the dragon night still holds the sky in its cold black coils?

Tell me, bird of the morning, how, through the twofold night of the sky and the leaves, he found his way into your dream, the messenger out of the east?

The world did not believe you when you cried. 'The sun is on his way, the night is no more.'

O sleeper, awake!

Bare your forehead, waiting for the first blessing of light, and sing with the bird of he morning in glad faith.

26

The beggar in me lifted his lean hands to the starless sky and cried into night's ear with his hungry voice.

His prayers were to the blind Darkness who lay like a fallen god in a desolate heaven of lost hopes.

The cry of desire eddied round a chasm of despair, a wailing bird circling its empty nest.

But when morning dropped anchor at the rim of the East, the beggar in me leapt and cried:

'Blessed am I that the deaf night denied me–that its coffer was empty.'

He cried, 'O Life, O Light, you are precious! and precious is the joy that at last has known you!'

27

Sanatan was telling his beads by the Ganges when a Brahmin in rags came to him and said, 'Help me, I am poor!'

'My alms-bowl is all this is my own,' said Sanatan, 'I have given away everything I had.'

'But my lord Shiva came to me in my dreams,' said the Brahmin, 'and counselled me to come to you.'

Sanatan suddenly remembered he had picked up a stone without price among the pebbles on the river-bank, and thinking that some one might need it hid it in the sands.

He pointed out the spot to the Brahmin, who wondering dug up the stone.

The Brahmin sat on the earth and mused alone till the sun went down behind the trees, and cowherds went home with their cattle.

Then he rose and came slowly to Sanatan and said, 'Master, give me the least fraction of the wealth that disdains all the wealth of the world.'

And he threw the precious stone into the water.

28

Time after time I came to your gate with raised hands, asking for more and yet more.
You gave and gave, now in slow measure, now in sudden excess.

I took some, and some things I let drop: some lay heavy on my hands; some I made into playthings and broke them when tired; till the wrecks and the hoard of your gifts grew immense, hiding you, and the ceaseless expectation wore my heart out.

Take, oh take–has now become my cry.

Shatter all from this beggar's bowl: put out this lamp of the importunate watcher: hold my hands, raise me from the still-gathering heap of your gifts into the bare infinity of your uncrowded presence.

29

You have set me among those who are defeated.

I know it is not for me to win, nor to leave the game.

I shall plunge into the pool although but to sink to the bottom.

I shall play the game of my undoing.

I shall stake all I have and when I lose my last penny I shall stake myself, and then I think I shall have won through my utter defeat.

30

A smile of mirth spread over the sky when you dressed my heart in rags and sent her forth into the road to beg.

She went from door to door, and many a time when her bowl was nearly full she was robbed.

At the end of the weary day she came to your palace gate holding up her pitiful bowl, and you came and took her hand and seated her beside you on your throne.

31

'Who among you will take up the duty of feeding the hungry?' Lord Buddha asked his followers when famine raged at Shravasti.

Ratnakar, the banker, hung his head and said, 'Much more is needed than all my wealth to feed the hungry.'

Jaysen, the chief of the King's army, said, 'I would gladly give my life's blood, but there is not enough food in my house.'

Dharmapal, who owned broad acres of land, said with a sigh, 'The drought demon has sucked my fields dry. I know not how to pay King's dues.'

Then rose Supriya, the mendicant's daughter.
She bowed to all and meekly said, 'I will feed the hungry.'

'How!' they cried in surprise. 'How can you hope to fulfil that vow?'

'I am the poorest of you all,' said Supriya, 'that is my strength. I have my coffer and my store at each of your houses.'

32

My king was unknown to me, therefore when he claimed his tribute I was bold to think I would hide myself leaving my debts unpaid.

I fled and fled behind my day's work and my night's dreams.

But his claims followed me at every breath I drew.

Thus I came to know that I am known to him and no place left which in mine.

Now I wish to lay my all before his feet, and gain the right to my place in his kingdom.

33

When I thought I would mould you, an image from my life for men to worship, I brought my dust and desires and all my coloured delusions and dreams.

When I asked you to mould with my life an image from your heart for you to love, you brought your fire and force, and truth, loveliness and peace.

34

'Sire', announced the servant to the King, 'the saint Narottam has never deigned to enter your royal temple.

'He is singing God's praise under the trees by the open road. The temple is empty of worshippers.

'They flock round him like bees round the white lotus, leaving the golden jar of honey unheeded.'

The king, vexed at heart, went to the spot where Narottam sat on the grass.

He asked him, 'Father, why leave my temple of the golden dome and sit on the dust outside to preach God's love?'

'Because God is not there in your temple,' said Narottam.

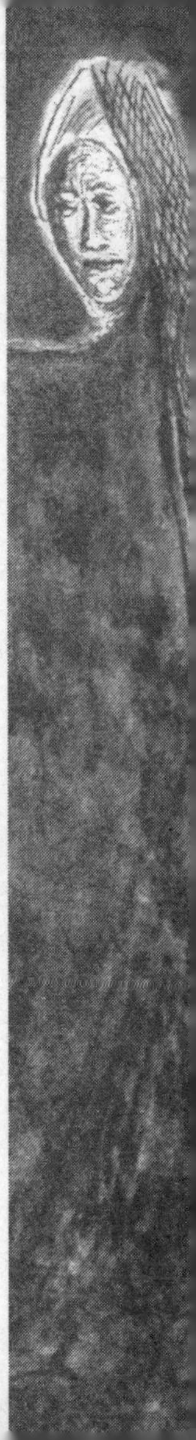

The King frowned and said, 'Do you know, twenty millions of gold went to the making of that marvel of art, and it was consecrated to God with costly rites?'

'Yes, I know it,' answered Narottam. 'It was in that year when thousands of your people whose houses had been burned stood vainly asking for help at your door.

'And God said, "The poor creature who can give no shelter to his brothers would build my house!"

'And he took his place with the shelterless under the trees by the road.

'And that golden bubble is empty of all but hot vapour of pride.'

The King cried in anger, 'Leave my land.'

Calmly said the saint, 'Yes, banish me where you have banished my God.'

35

The trumpet lies is the dust.
The wind is weary, the light is dead.
Ah the evil day!
Come, fighters, carrying your flags, and singers, with your war-songs!
Come, pilgrims of the march, hurrying on your journey!
The trumpet lies in the dust waiting for us.

I was on my way to the temple with my evening offerings, seeking for a place of rest after the day's dusty toil: hoping my hurts would be healed and the stains in my garment washed white, when I found thy trumpet lying in the dust.
Was it not the hour for me to light my evening lamp?
Had not the night sung its lullaby to the stars?
O thou blood-red rose, my poppies of sleep have paled and faded!
I was certain my wanderings were over and my debts all paid when suddenly I came upon thy trumpet lying in the dust.

Strike my drowsy heart with thy spell of youth!
Let my joy in life blaze up in fire.
Let the shafts of awakening fly through the heart of night, and a thrill of dread shake blindness and palsy.
I have come to raise thy trumpet from the dust.
Sleep is no more for me–my walk shall be through showers of arrows.
Some shall run out of their houses and come to my side–some shall weep.
Some in their beds shall toss and groan in dire dreams.
For to-night they trumpet shall be sounded.

From thee I have asked peace only to find shame.
Now I stand before thee–help me to put on my armour!
Let hard blows of trouble strike fire into my life.
Let my heart beat in pain, the drum of thy victory.
My hands shall be utterly emptied to take up thy trumpet.

36

When, mad in their mirth, they raised dust to soil thy robe, O Beautiful, it made my heart sick.

I cried to thee and said, 'Take thy rod of punishment and judge them.'

The morning light struck upon those eyes, red with the revel of night; the place of the white lily greeted their burning breath; the stars through the depth of the sacred dark stared at their carousing–at those that raised due to soil thy robe, O Beautiful!

Thy judgement seat was in the flower garden, in the birds' notes in springtime: in the shady river-banks, where the trees muttered in answer to the muttering of the waves.

O my Lover, they were pitiless in their passion.

They prowled in the dark to snatch thy ornaments to deck their own desires.

When they had struck thee and thou wert pained, it pierced me to the quick, and I cried to thee and said,

'Take thy sword, O my Lover, and judge them!'

Ah, but thy justice was vigilant.

A mother's tears were shed on their insolence; the imperishable faith of a lover hid their spears of rebellion in its own wounds.

Thy judgement was in the mute pain of sleepless love: in the blush of the chaste: in the tears of the night of the desolate: in the pale morning-light of forgiveness.

O Terrible, they in their reckless greed climbed thy gate at night, breaking into thy storehouse to rob thee.

But the weight of their plunder grew immense, too heavy to carry or to remove.

Thereupon I cried to thee and said, Forgive them, O Terrible!

Thy forgiveness burst in storms, throwing them down, scattering their thefts in the dust.

Thy forgiveness was in the thunder-stone; in the shower of blood; in the angry red of the sunset.

37

Upagupta, the disciple of Buddha, lay asleep on the dust by the city wall of Mathura.

Lamps were all out, doors were all shut, and stars were all hidden by the murky sky of August.

Whose feet were those tinkling with anklets, touching his breast of a sudden?

He woke up startled, and the light from a woman's lamp struck his forgiving eyes.

It was the dancing girl, starred with jewels, clouded with a pale-blue mantle, drunk with the wine of her youth.

She lowered her lamp and saw the young face, austerely beautiful. 'Forgive me, young ascetic,' said the woman; 'graciously come to my house. The dusty earth is not a fit bed for you.'

The ascetic answered, 'Woman, go on your way; when the time is ripe I will come to you.'

Suddenly the black night showed its teeth in a flash of lightning.

The storm growled from the corner of the sky, and the woman trembled in fear.

The branches of the wayside trees were aching with blossom.

Gay notes of the flute came floating in the warm spring air from afar.

The citizens had gone to the woods, to the festival of flowers.

From the mid-sky gazed the full moon on the shadows of the silent town.

The young ascetic was walking in the lonely street, while overhead the lovesick *koels* urged from the mango branches their sleepless plaint.

Upagupta passed through the city gates, and stood at the base of the rampart.

What woman lay in the shadow of the wall at his feet, struck with the black pestilence, her body spotted with sores, hurriedly driven away from the town?

The ascetic sat by her side, taking her head on his knees, and moistened her lips with water and smeared her body with balm.

'Who are you, merciful one?' asked the woman.

'The time, at last, has come to visit you, and I am here.' Replied the young ascetic.

38

This is no mere dallying of love between us, my lover.

Again and again have swooped down upon me the screaming nights of storm, blowing out my lamp: dark doubts have gathered, blotting out all stars from my sky.

Again and again the banks have burst, letting the flood sweep away my harvest, and wailing and despair have rent my sky from end to end.

This have I learnt that there are blows of pain in your love, never the cold apathy of death.

39

The wall breaks asunder, light, like divine laughter, bursts in.

Victory, O Light!

The heart of the night is pierced!

With your flashing sword cut in twain the tangle of doubt and feeble desires!

Victory!

Come, Implacable!

Come, you who are terrible in your whiteness.

O Light, your drum sounds in the march of fire, and the red torch is held on high; death dies in a burst of splendour!

40

O Fire, my brother, I sing victory to you.

You are the bright red image of fearful freedom.

You swing your arms in the sky, you sweep your impetuous fingers across the harp-string, your dance music is beautiful.

When my days are ended and the gates are opened you will burn to ashes this cordage of hands and feet. My body will be one with you, my heart will be caught in the whirls of your frenzy, and the burning heart that was my life will flash up and mingle itself in your flame.

41

The Boatman is out crossing the wild sea at night.
The mast is aching because of its full sails filled with the violent wind.
Stung with the night's fang the sky falls upon the sea, poisoned with black fear.

The waves dash their head against the dark unseen, and the Boatman is out crossing the wild sea.

The Boatman is out, I know not for what tryst, startling the night with the sudden white of his sails.
I know not at what shore, at last, he lands to reach the silent courtyard where the lamp is burning and to find her who sits in the dust and waits.
What is the quest that makes his boat care not for storm nor darkness?
Is it heavy with gems and pearls?
Ah, no, the Boatman brings with him no treasure, but only a white rose in his hand and a song on his lips.

It is for her who watches alone at night with her lamp burning.

She dwells in the wayside hut.
Her loose hair flies in the wind and hides her eyes.
The storm shrieks through her broken doors, the light flickers in her earthen lamp flinging shadows on the walls.
Through the howl of the winds she hears him call her name, she whose name is unknown.
It is long since the Boatman sailed.

It will be long before the day breaks and he knocks at the door.
The drums will not be beaten and none will know;.
Only light shall fill the house, blessed shall be the dust, and the heart glad.
All doubts shall vanish in silence when the Boatman comes to the shore.

42

I cling to this living raft, my body, in the narrow stream of my earthly years. I leave it when the crossing is over.

And then?

I do not know if the light there and the darkness are the same.

The Unknown is the perpetual freedom:

He is pitiless in his love.

He crushes the shell for the pearl, dumb in the prison of the dark.

You muse and weep for the days that are done, poor heart!

Be glad that days are to come!

The hour strikes, O pilgrim!

It is time for you to take the parting of the ways!

His face will be unveiled once again and you shall meet.

43

Over the relic of Lord Buddha King Bimbisar built, a shrine, a salutation in white marble.

There in the evening would come all the brides and daughters of the King's house to offer flowers and light lamps.

When the son became king in his time he washed his father's creed away with blood, and lit sacrificial fires with its sacred books.

The autumn day was dying.

The evening hour of worship was near.

Shrimati, the queen's maid, devoted to Lord Buddha, having bathed in holy water, and decked the golden tray with lamps and fresh white blossoms, silently raised her dark eyes to the queen's face.

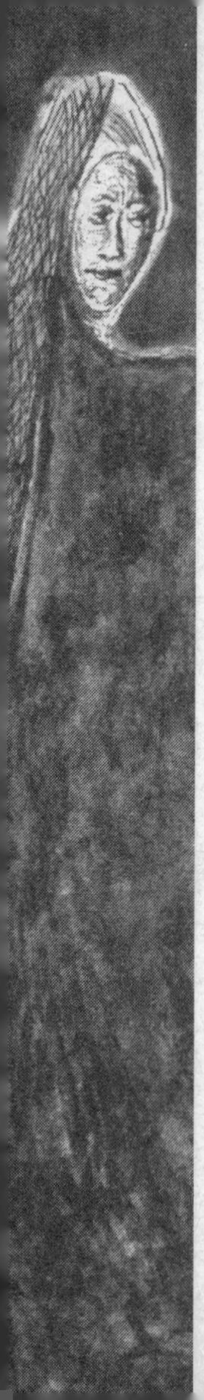

The queen shuddered in fear and said, “Do you not know, foolish girl, that death is the penalty for whoever brings worship to Buddha’s shrine?

‘Such is the King’s will.’

Shrimati bowed to the queen, and turning away from her door came and stood before Amita, the newly wed bride of the King’s son.

A mirror of burnished gold on her lap, the newly wed bride was braiding her dark long tresses and painting the red spot of good luck at the parting of her hair.

Her hands trembled when she saw the young maid, and she cried.

‘What fearful peril would you bring me! Leave me this instant.’

Princess Shukla sat at the window reading her book of romance by the light of the setting sun.

She started when she saw at her door the maid with the sacred offerings.

Her book fell down from her lap, and she whispered in Shrimati's ears, 'Rush not to death, daring woman."

Shrimati walked from door to door.

She raised her head and cried, 'O women of the king's house, hasten!

'The time for our Lord's worship is come!'

Some shut their doors in her face and some reviled her.

The last gleam of daylight faded from the bronze dome of the palace tower.

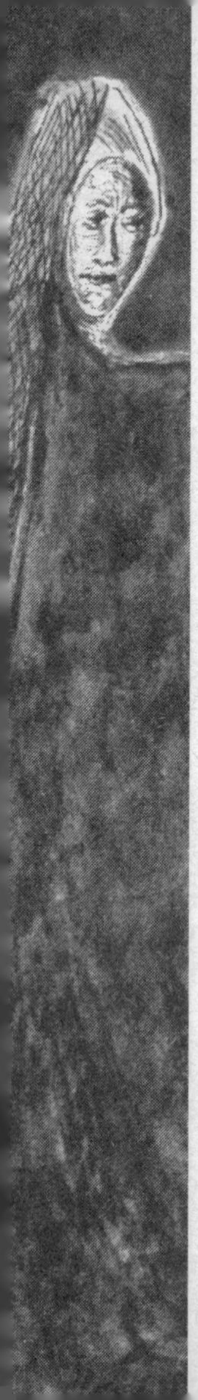

Deep shadows settled in street corners; the bustle of the city was hushed: the gong at the temple of Shiva announced the time of the evening prayer.

In the dark of the autumn evening, deep as a limpid lake, stars throbbed with light, when the guards of the palace garden were startled to see through the trees a row of lamps burning at the shrine of Buddha.

They ran with their swords unsheathed, crying, 'Who are you, foolish one, reckless of death?'

'I am Shrimati,' replied a sweet voice, 'the servant of Lord Buddha.'

The next moment her heart's blood coloured the cold marble with its red.

And in the still hour of stars died the light of the last lamp of worship at the foot of the shrine.

44

The day that stands between you and me makes her last bow of farewell.

The night draws her veil over her face, and hides the one lamp burning in my chamber.

Your dark servant comes noiselessly and spreads the bridal carpet for you to take your seat there alone with me in the wordless silence till night is done.

45

My night has passed on the bed of sorrow, and my eyes are tired. My heavy heart is not yet ready to meet morning with its crowded joys.

Draw a veil over this naked light, beckon aside from me this glaring flash and dance of life.

Let thy mantle of tender darkness cover me in its folds, and cover my pain awhile from the pressure of the world.

46

The time is past when I could repay her for all that I received.

Her night has found its morning and thou hast taken her to thy arms: and to thee I bring my gratitude and my gifts that were for her.

For all hurts and offences to her I come to thee for forgiveness.

I offer to thy service those flowers of my love that remained in bud when she waited for them to open.

47

I found a few old letters of mine carefully hidden in her box—a few small toys for her memory to play with.

With a timorous heart she tried to steal these trifles from time's turbulent stream, and said, 'These are mine only!'

Ah, there is no one now to claim them, who can pay their price with loving care, yet here they are still.

Surely there is love in his world to save her from utter loss, even like this love of hers that saved these letters with such fond care.

48

Bring beauty and order into my forlorn life, woman, as you brought them into my house when you lived.

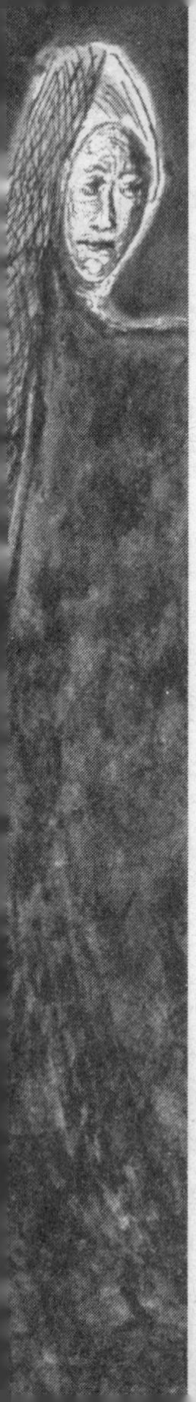

Sweep away the dusty fragments of the hours, fill the empty jars, and mend all that has been neglected.

Then open the inner door of the shrine, light the candle, and let us meet there in silence before our God.

49

The pain was great when the strings were being tuned, my Master!

Begin your music, and let me forget the pain; let me feel in beauty what you had in your mind through those pitiless days.

The waning night lingers at my doors, let her take her leave in songs.

Pour your heart into my life strings, my Master, in tunes that descend from your stars.

50

In the lightning flash of a moment I have seen the immensity of your creation in my life—creation through many a death from world to world.

I weep at my unworthiness when I see my life in the hands of the unmeaning hours,—but when I see it in your hands I know it is too precious to be squandered among shadows.

51

I know that at the dim end of some day the sun will bid me its last farewell.

Shepherds will play their pipers beneath the banyan trees, and cattle graze on the slope by the river, while my days will pass into the dark.

This is my prayer, that I may know before I leave why the earth called me to her arms.

Why her night's silence spoke to me of stars, and her daylight kissed my thoughts into flower.

Before I go may I linger over my last refrain, completing its music, may the lamp be lit to see your face and the wreath woven to crown you.

52

What music is that in whose measure the world is rocked?

We laugh when it beats upon the crest of life, we shrink in terror when it returns into the dark.

But the play is the same that comes and goes with the rhythm of the endless music.

You hide your treasure in the palm of your hand, and we cry that we are robbed.

But open and shut your palm as you will, the gain and the loss are the same.

At the game you play with your own self you lose and win at once.

53

I have kissed this world with my eyes and my limbs; I have wrapt it within my heart in numberless folds; I have flooded its days and nights with thoughts till the world and my life have grown one,—and I love my life because I love the light of the sky to enwoven with me.

If to leave this world be as real as to love it—then there must be a meaning in the meeting and the parting of life.

If that were deceived in death, then the canker of this deceit would eat into all things, and the stars would shrivel and grow black.

54

The cloud said to me, 'I vanish'; the Night said, 'I plunge into the fiery dawn.'

The Pain said, 'I remain in deep silence as his footprint.'

'I die into the fulness,' said my life to me.

The Earth said, 'My lights kiss your thoughts every moment.'

'The days pass,' Love said, 'but I wait for you.'

Death said, 'I ply the boat of your life across the sea.'

55

Tulsidas, the poet, was wandering, deep in thought, by the Ganges, in that lonely spot where they burn their dead.

He found a woman sitting at the feet of the corpse of her dead husband, gaily dressed as for a wedding.

She rose as she saw him, bowed to him, and said, 'Permit me, Master, with your blessing, to follow my husband to heaven.'

'Why such hurry, my daughter?' asked Tulsidas. 'Is not this earth also His who made heaven?'

'For heaven I do not long,' said the woman. 'I want my husband.'

Tulsidas smiled and said to her, 'Go back to your home, my child. Before the month is over you will find your husband.'

The woman went back with glad hope. Tulsidas came to her every day and gave her high thoughts to think, till her heart was filled to the brim with divine love.

When the month was scarcely over, her neighbours came to her, asking. 'Woman, have you found your husband?'

The widow smiled and said, 'I have.'

Eagerly they asked, 'Where is he?'

'In my heart is my lord, one with me,' said the woman.

56

You came for a moment to my side and touched me with the great mystery of the woman that there is in the heart of creation.

She who is ever returning to God his own out flowing of sweetness; she is the ever fresh beauty and youth in nature; she dances in the bubbling streams and sings in the morning light; she with heaving suckles the thirsty earth; in her the Eternal One breaks in two in a joy that no longer may contain itself, and overflows in the pain of love.

57

Who is she who dwells in my heart, the woman forlorn for ever?'

I wooed her and I failed to win her.

I decked her with wreaths and sang in her praise.

A smile shone in her face for a moment, then it faded.

'I have no joy in thee,' she cried, the woman in sorrow.

I bought her jewelled anklets and fanned her with a fan gem-studded; I made her a bed on a bedstead of gold.

There flickered a gleam of gladness in her eyes, then it died.

'I have no joy in these,' she cried, the woman in sorrow.

I seated her upon a car of triumph and drove her from end to end of the earth.

Conquered hearts bowed down at her feet, and shouts of applause rang in the sky.

Pride shone in her eyes for a moment, then it was dimmed in tears.

'I have no joy in conquest,' she cried, the woman in sorrow.

I asked her, 'Tell me whom do you seek?'

She only said, 'I wait for him of the unknown name.'

Days pass by and she cries, 'When will my beloved come whom I know not, and be known to me for ever?'

58

Yours is the light that breaks forth from the dark, and the good that sprouts from the cleft heart of strife.

Yours is the house that opens upon the world, and the love that calls to the battlefield.

Yours is the gift that still is a gain when everything is a loss, and the life that flows through the caverns of death.

Yours is the heaven that lies in the common dust, and you are there for me, you are there for all.

59

When the weariness of the road is upon me, and the thirst of the sultry day; when the ghostly hours of the dusk throw their shadows across my life, then I cry not for your voice only, my friend, but for your touch.

There is an anguish in my heart for the burden of its riches not given to you.

Put out your hand through the night, let me hold it and fill it and keep it; let me feel its touch along the lengthening stretch of my loneliness.

60

The odour cries in the bud, 'Ah me, the day departs, the happy day of spring, and I am a prisoner in petals!' Do not lose heart timid thing!

Your bonds will burst, the bud will open into flower, and when you die in the fulness of life, even then the spring will live on.

The odour pants and flutters within the bud, crying,
'Ah me, the hours pass by, yet I do not know where I go, or what it is I seek!'
Do not lose heart, timid thing!
The spring breeze has overheard your desire, the day will not end before you have fulfilled your being.

Dark is the future to her, and the odour cries in despair,
'Ah me, through whose fault is my life so unmeaning?
'Who can tell me, why I am at all?'
Do not lose heart, timid thing!
The perfect dawn is near when you will mingle your life with all life and know at last your purpose.

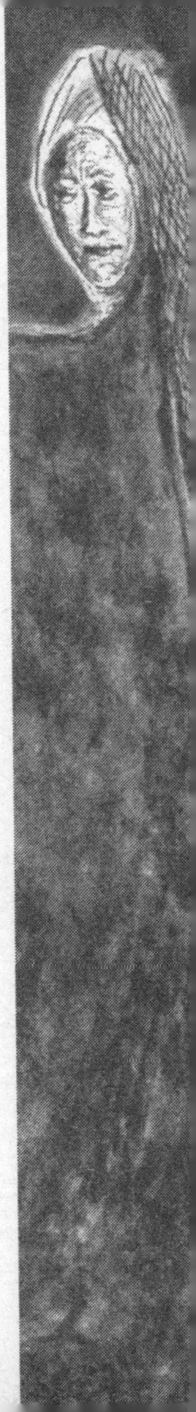

61

She is still, a child, my lord.

She runs about your palace and plays, and tries to make of you a plaything as well.

She heeds not when her hair tumbles down and her careless garment drags in the dust.

She falls asleep when you speak to her and answers not—and the flower you give her in the morning slips to the dust from her hands.

When the storm bursts and darkness is over the sky she is sleepless; her dolls lie scattered on the earth and she clings to you in terror.

She is afraid that she may fail in service to you.

But with a smile you watch her at her game.

You know her.

The child sitting in the dust is your destined bride; her play will be stilled and deepened into love.

62

'What is there but the sky, O Sun, that can hold thine image?'

'I dream of thee, but to serve thee I can never hope,' the dewdrop wept and said, 'I am too small to take thee unto me, great lord, and my life is all tears.'

'I illumine the limitless sky, yet I can yield myself up to a tiny drop of drew,' thus the Sun said; 'I shall become but a sparkle of light and fill you, and your little life will be a laughing orb.'

63

Not for me is the love that knows no restraint, but like the foaming wine that having burst its vessel in a moment would run to waste.

Send me the love which is cool and pure like your rain that blesses the thirsty earth and fills the homely earthen jars.

Send me the love that would soak down into the centre of being, and from there would spread like the unseen sap through the branching tree of life, giving birth to fruits and flowers.

Send me the love that keeps the heart still with the fulness of peace.

64

The sun had set on the western margin of the river among the tangle of the forest.

The hermit boys had brought the cattle home, and sat round the fire to listen to the master, Gautama, when a strange boy came, and greeted him with fruits and flowers, and, bowing low at his feet, spoke in a bird-like voice—'Lord, I have come to thee to be taken into the path of the supreme Truth.

'My name is Satyakama.'

'Blessings be on thy head,' said the master.

'Of what clan art thou, my child? It is only fitting for a Brahmin to aspire to the highest wisdom.'

'Master,' answered the boy, 'I know not of what clan I am. I shall go and ask my mother.'

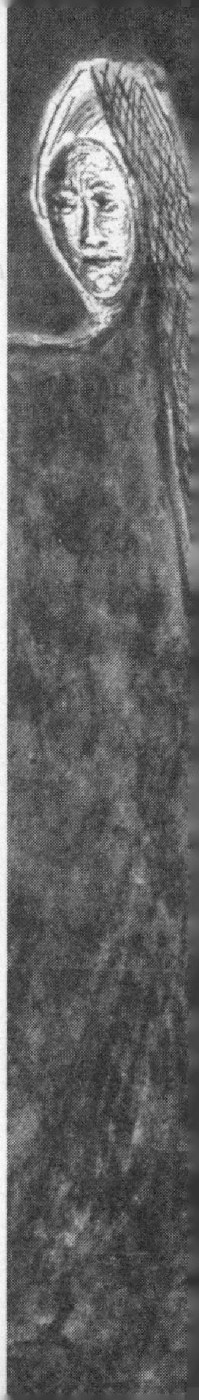

Thus saying, Satyakama took leave, and wading across the shallow stream, came back to his mother's hut, which stood at the end of the sandy waste at the edge of the sleeping village.

The lamp burnt dimly in the room, and the mother stood at the door in the dark waiting for her son's return.

She clasped him to her bosom, kissed him on his hair, and asked him of his errand to the master.

'What is the name of my father, dear mother?' asked the boy.

'It is only fitting for a Brahmin to aspire to the highest wisdom, said Lord Gautama to me.'

The woman lowered her eyes, and spoke in a whisper.

'In my youth I was poor and had many masters. Thou didst come to thy mother Jabala's arms, my darling, who had no husband.'

The early rays of the sun glistened on the tree-tops of the forest hermitage.

The students, with their tangled hair still wet with their morning bath, sat under the ancient tree, before the master.

There came Satyakama.

He bowed low at the feet of the sage, and stood silent.

'Tell me,' the great teacher asked him, 'of what clan art thou?'

'My lord,' he answered, 'I know it not. My mother said when I asked her, "I had served many masters in my youth, and thou hadst come to thy mother Jabala's arms, who had no husband."'

There rose a murmur like the angry hum of bees disturbed in their hive; and the students muttered at the shameless insolence of that outcast. Master Gautama rose from his seat, stretched out his arms, took the boy to his bosom, and said, 'Best of all Brahmins art thou, my child. Thou hast the noblest heritage of truth.'

65

May be there is one house in this city where the gate opens for ever this morning at the touch of the sunrise, where the errand of the light is fulfilled.

The flowers have opened in hedges and gardens, and may be there is one heart that has found in them this morning the gift that has been on its voyage from endless time.

66

Listen, my heart, in his flute is the music of the smell of wild flowers, of the glist4ening leaves and gleaming water, of shadows resonant with bees' wings.

The flute steals his smile from my friend's lips and spreads it over my life.

67

You always stand alone beyond the stream of my songs.

The waves of my tunes wash your feet but I know not how to reach them.

This play of mine with you is a play from afar.

It is the pain of separation that melts into melody through my flute.

I wait for the time when your boat crosses over to my shore and you take my flute into your own hands.

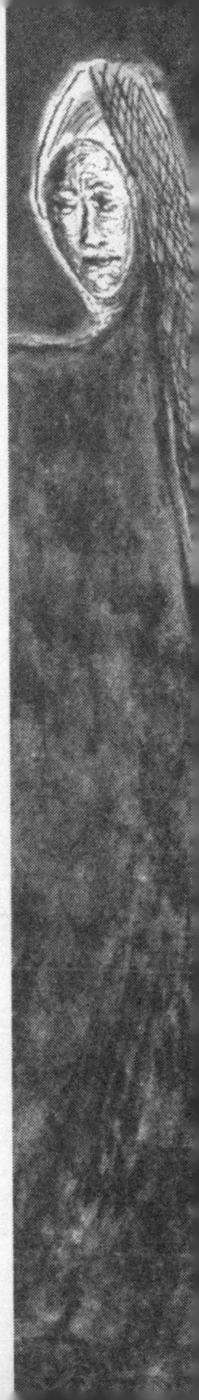

68

Suddenly the window of my heart flew open this morning, the window that looks out on your heart. I wondered to see that the name by which you know me is written in April leaves and flowers, and I sat silent.

The curtain was blown away for a moment between my songs and yours.

I found that your morning light was full of my own mute songs unsung; I thought that I would learn them at your feet—and I sat silent.

69

You were in the centre of my heart, therefore when my heart wandered she never found you; you hid yourself from my loves and hopes till the last, for you were always in them.

You were he inmost joy in the play of my youth, and when I was too busy with the play the joy was passed by.

You sang to me in the ecstasies of my life and I forgot to sing to you.

70

When you hold your lamp in the sky it throws its light on my face and its shadow falls over you.

When I hold the lamp of love in my heart its light falls on you and I am left standing behind in the shadow.

71

O the waves, the sky-devouring waves, glistening with light, dancing with life, the waves of eddying joy, rushing for ever.

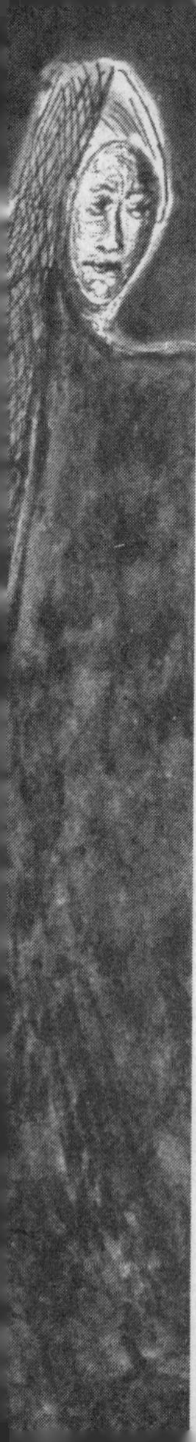

The stars rock upon them, thoughts of every tint are cast up out of the deep and scattered on the beach of life.

Birth and death rise and fall with their rhythm, and the sea-gull of my heart spreads its wings crying in delight.

72

The joy ran from all the world to build my body.

The lights of the skies kissed and kissed her till she woke.

Flowers of hurrying summers sighed in her breath and voices of winds and water sang in her movements.

The passion of the tide of colours in clouds and in forests flowed into her life, and the music of all things caressed her limbs into shape.

She is my bride,–she has lighted her lamp in my house.

73

The spring with its leaves and flowers has come into my body.

The bees hum there the morning long, and the winds idly play with the shadows.

A sweet fountain springs up from the heart of my heart.

My eyes are washed with delight like the dew-bathed morning, and life is quivering in all my limbs like the sounding strings of the lute.

Are you wandering alone by the shore of my life, where the tide is in flood. O lover of my endless days?

Are my dreams flitting round you like the moths with their many-coloured wings?

And are those your songs that are echoing in the dark caves of my being?

Who but you can hear the hum of the crowded hours that sounds in my veins to-day, the glad steps that dance in my breast, the clamour of the restless life beating its wings in my body?

74

My bonds are cut, my debts are paid, my door has been opened, I go everywhere.

They crouch in their corner and weave their web of pale hours, they count their coins sitting in the dust and call me back.

But my sword is forged, my armour is put on, my horse is eager to run.
I shall win my kingdom.

75

It was only the other day that I came to your earth, naked and nameless, with a wailing cry.

To-day my voice is glad, while you, my lord, stand aside to make room that I may fill my life.

Even when I bring you my songs for an offering I have the secret hope that men will come and love me for them.

You love to discover that I love this world where you have brought me.

76

Timidly I cowered in the shadow of safety, but now, when the surge of joy carries my heart upon its crest, my heart clings to the cruel rock of its trouble.

I sat alone in a corner of my house thinking it too narrow for any guest, but now when its door is flung open by an unbidden joy I find there is room for thee and for all the world.

I walked upon tiptoe, careful of my person, perfumed, and adorned—but now when a glad whirlwind has overthrown me in the dust I laugh and roll on the earth at thy feet like a child.

77

The world is yours at once and for ever.

And because you have no want, my king, you have no pleasure in your wealth.

It is as though it were naught.

Therefore through slow time you give me what is yours, and ceaselessly win your kingdom in me.

Day after day you buy your sunrise from my heart, and you find your love carven into the image of my life.

78

To the birds you gave songs, the birds gave you songs in return.

You gave me only voice, yet asked for more, and I sing.

You made your winds light and they are fleet in their service. You burdened my hands that I myself may lighten them, and at last, gain unburdened freedom for your service.

You created your Earth filling its shadows with fragments of light.

Their you paused; you left me empty-handed in the dust to create your heaven.

To all things else you give; from me you ask.

The harvest of my life ripens in the sun and the shower till I reap more than you sowed, gladdening your heart, O Master of the golden granary.

79

Let me not pray to be sheltered from dangers but to be fearless in facing them.

Let me not beg for the stilling of my pain but for the heart to conquer it.

Let me not look for allies in life's battlefield but to my own strength.

Let me not crave in anxious fear to be saved but hope for the patience to win my freedom.

Grant me that I may not be a coward, feeling your mercy in my success alone; but let me find the grasp of your hand in my failure.

80

You did not know yourself when you dwelt alone, and there was no crying of an errand when the wind ran from the hither to the farther shore.

I came and you woke, and the skies blossomed with lights.

You made me open in many flowers; rocked me in the cradles of many forms; hid me in death and found me again in life.

I came and your heart heaved; pain came to you and joy.

You touched me and tingled into love.

But in my eyes there is film of shame and in my breast a flicker of fear; my face is veiled and I weep when I cannot see you.

Yet I know the endless thirst in your heart for sight of me, the thirst that cries at my door in the repeated knockings of sunrise.

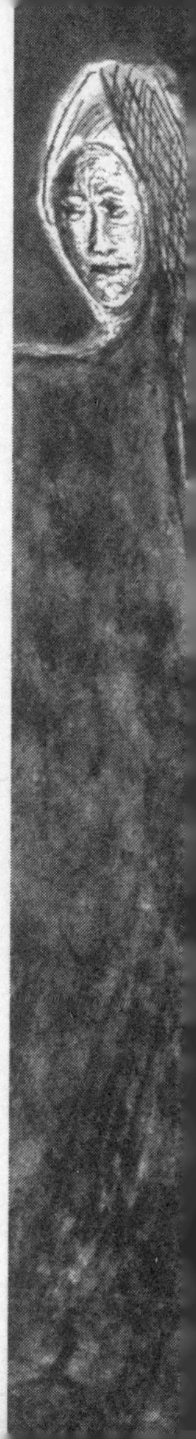

81

You in your timeless watch, listen to my approaching steps, while your gladness gathers in the morning twilight and breaks in the burst of light.

The nearer I draw to you the deeper grows the fervour in the dance of the sea.

Your world is a branching spray of light filling your hands, but your heaven is in my secret heart; it slowly opens its buds in shy love.

82

I will utter your name, sitting alone among the shadows of my silent thoughts.

I will utter it without words, I will utter it without purpose.

For I am like a child that calls its mother an hundred times, glad that it can say 'Mother.'

83

I

I feel that all the stars shine in me.

The world breaks into my life like a flood.

The flowers blossom in my body.

All the youthfulness of land and water smokes like an incense in my heart; and the breath of all things plays on my thoughts as on a flute.

II

When the world sleeps I come to your door.

The stars are silent, and I am afraid to sing.

I wait and watch, till your shadow passes by the balcony of night and I return with a full heart.

Then in the morning I sing by the roadside;

The flowers in the hedge give me answer and the morning air listens,

The travellers suddenly stop and look in my face, thinking I have called them by their names.

III

Keep me at your door ever attending to your wishes, and let me go about in your Kingdom accepting your call.

Let me not sink and disappear in the depth of langour.

Let not my life be worn out to tatters by penury of waste.

Let not those doubts encompass me,—the dust of distractions.

Let me not pursue many paths to gather many things. Let me not bend my heart to the yoke of the many. Let me hold my head high in the courage and pride of being your servant.

84

The Oarsmen

Do you hear the tumult of death afar,
The call midst the fire-floods and poisonous clouds.
– The Captain's call to the steersman to turn the ship to an unnamed shore,
For that time is over–the stagnant time in the port–
Where the same old merchandise is bought and sold in an endless round,
Where dead things drift in the exhaustion and emptiness of truth.

They wake up in sudden fear and ask,
'Comrades, what hour has struck?
When shall the dawn begin?'
The clouds have blotted away the stars–
Who is there then can see the beckoning finger of the day?

They run out with oars in hand, the beds are emptied,
the mother prays, the wife watches by the door;
There is a wail of parting that rises to the sky,
And there is the Captain's voice in the dark:
'Come, sailors, for the time in the harbour is over!'

All the black evils in the world have overflowed their banks,
Yet, oarsmen, take your places with the blessing of sorrow in your souls!
Whom do you blame brothers? Bow your heads down!
The sin has been yours and ours.
The heat growing in the heart of God for ages—
The cowardice of the weak, the arrogance of the strong,
the greed of fat prosperity, the rancour of the wronged,
pride of race, and insult to man—
Has burst God's peace, raging in storm.

Like a ripe pod, let the tempest break its heart into pieces, scattering thunders.

Stop your bluster of dispraise and of self-praise,
And with the calm of silent prayer on your foreheads sail to that unnamed shore.

We have, known sins and evils every day and death we have known;
They pass over our world like clouds mocking us with their transient lightning laughter.
Suddenly they have stopped, become a prodigy,
And men must stand before them saying:
'We do not fear you, O Monster! for we have lived every day by conquering you,
'And we die with the faith that Peace is true, and Good is true, and true is the eternal One!'

If the Deathless dwell not in the heart of death,
If glad wisdom bloom not bursting the sheath of sorrow,
If sin do not die of its own revealment,
If pride break not under its load of decorations,

Then whence comes the hope that drives these men from their homes like stars rushing to their death in the morning light?
Shall the value of the martyrs' blood and mothers' tears be utterly lost in the dust of the earth, not buying Heaven with their price?
And when Man bursts his mortals bounds, is not the Boundless revealed that moment?

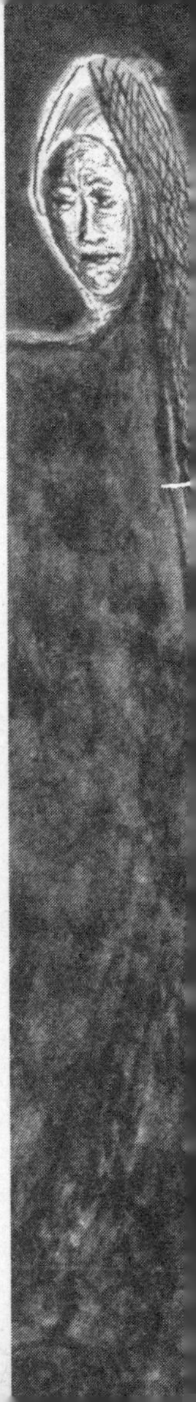

85

The Song of the Defeated

My master has bid me while I stand at the roadside, to sing the song of Defeat, for that is the bride whom He woos in secret.

She has put on the dark veil, hiding her face from the crowd, but the jewel glows on her breast in the dark.

She is forsaken of the day, and God's night is waiting for her with its lamps lighted and flowers wet with dew.

She is silent with her eyes downcast; she has left her home behind her, from her home has come that wailing in the wind.

But the stars are singing the love-song of the eternal to a face sweet with shame and suffering.

The door has been opened in the lonely chamber, the call has sounded, and the heart of the darkness throbs with awe because of the coming tryst.

86

Thanksgiving

Those who walk on the path of pride crushing the lowly life under their tread, covering the tender green of the earth with their footprints in blood;

Let them rejoice, and thank thee, Lord, for the day is theirs.

But I am thankful that my lot lies with the humble who suffer and bear the burden of power, and hide their faces and stifle their sobs in the dark.

For every throb of their pain has pulsed in the secret depth of thy night, and every insult has been gathered into thy great silence.

And the morrow is theirs.

O Sun, rise upon the bleeding hearts blossoming in flowers of the morning, and the torchlight revelry of pride shrunken to ashes.

notes

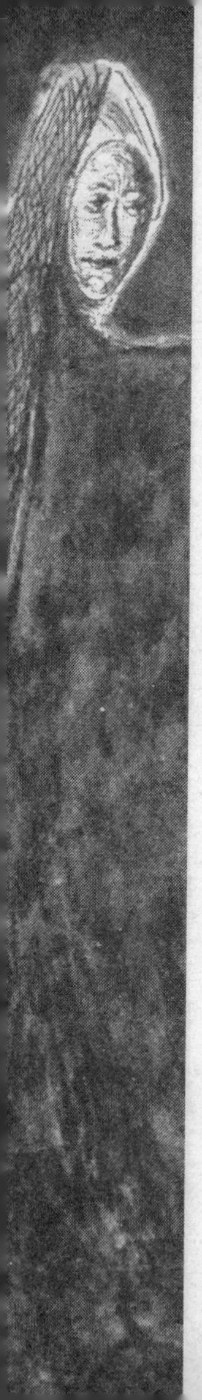

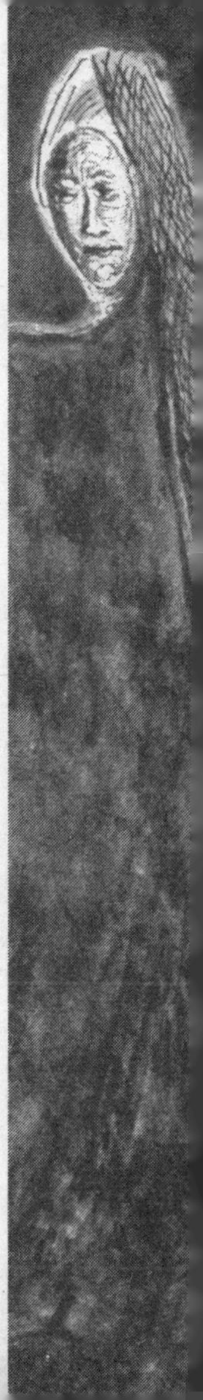